Published by Angelis Publications
ISBN: 978-0-9956516-0-9
www.angelispublications.com
Cover Design: Angie J Anderson

Welcome

 Enjoy your stay! 

Date	Name	Where we are from

Comments & what we especially enjoyed & recommend

Date	Name	Where we are from

Comments & what we especially enjoyed & recommend

Date	Name	Where we are from

Comments & what we especially enjoyed & recommend

Date	Name	Where we are from

Comments & what we especially enjoyed & recommend

Date	Name	Where we are from

Comments & what we especially enjoyed & recommend

Date	Name	Where we are from

Comments & what we especially enjoyed & recommend

Date	Name	Where we are from

Comments & what we especially enjoyed & recommend

Date	Name	Where we are from

Comments & what we especially enjoyed & recommend

Date	Name	Where we are from

Comments & what we especially enjoyed & recommend

Date	Name	Where we are from

Comments & what we especially enjoyed & recommend

Date	Name	Where we are from

Comments & what we especially enjoyed & recommend

Date	Name	Where we are from

Comments & what we especially enjoyed & recommend

Date	Name	Where we are from

Comments & what we especially enjoyed & recommend

Date	Name	Where we are from

Comments & what we especially enjoyed & recommend

Date	Name	Where we are from

Comments & what we especially enjoyed & recommend

Date	Name	Where we are from

Comments & what we especially enjoyed & recommend

Date	Name	Where we are from

Comments & what we especially enjoyed & recommend

Date	Name	Where we are from

Comments & what we especially enjoyed & recommend

Date	Name	Where we are from

Comments & what we especially enjoyed & recommend

Date	Name	Where we are from

Comments & what we especially enjoyed & recommend

Date	Name	Where we are from

Comments & what we especially enjoyed & recommend

Date	Name	Where we are from

Comments & what we especially enjoyed & recommend

Date	Name	Where we are from

Comments & what we especially enjoyed & recommend

Date	Name	Where we are from

Comments & what we especially enjoyed & recommend

Date	Name	Where we are from

Comments & what we especially enjoyed & recommend

Date	Name	Where we are from

Comments & what we especially enjoyed & recommend

Date	Name	Where we are from

Comments & what we especially enjoyed & recommend

Date	Name	Where we are from

Comments & what we especially enjoyed & recommend

Date	Name	Where we are from

Comments & what we especially enjoyed & recommend

Date	Name	Where we are from

Comments & what we especially enjoyed & recommend

Date	Name	Where we are from

Comments & what we especially enjoyed & recommend

Date	Name	Where we are from

Comments & what we especially enjoyed & recommend

Date	Name	Where we are from

Comments & what we especially enjoyed & recommend

Date	Name	Where we are from

Comments & what we especially enjoyed & recommend

Date	Name	Where we are from

Comments & what we especially enjoyed & recommend

Date	Name	Where we are from

Comments & what we especially enjoyed & recommend

Date	Name	Where we are from

Comments & what we especially enjoyed & recommend

Date	Name	Where we are from

Comments & what we especially enjoyed & recommend

Date	Name	Where we are from

Comments & what we especially enjoyed & recommend

Date	Name	Where we are from

Comments & what we especially enjoyed & recommend

Date	Name	Where we are from

Comments & what we especially enjoyed & recommend

Date	Name	Where we are from

Comments & what we especially enjoyed & recommend

Date	Name	Where we are from

Comments & what we especially enjoyed & recommend

Date	Name	Where we are from

Comments & what we especially enjoyed & recommend

Date	Name	Where we are from

Comments & what we especially enjoyed & recommend

Date	Name	Where we are from

Comments & what we especially enjoyed & recommend

Date	Name	Where we are from

Comments & what we especially enjoyed & recommend

Date	Name	Where we are from

Comments & what we especially enjoyed & recommend

www.ingramcontent.com/pod-product-compliance
Lightning Source LLC
Chambersburg PA
CBHW080810020826
48982CB00018B/987

9780995651609